THE PORTAGE POETRY SERIES

SERIES TITLES

A Bright Wound
Sarah A. Etlinger

The Velvet Book
Rae Gouirand

Listening to Mars
Sally Ashton

Glitter City
Bonnie Jill Emanuel

The Trouble with Being a Childless Only Child
Michelle Meyer

Happy Everything
Caitlin Cowan

Dear Lo
Brady Bove

Sadness of the Apex Predator
Dion O'Reilly

Do Not Feed the Animal
Hikari Miya

The Watching Sky
Judy Brackett Crowe

Let It Be Told in a Single Breath
Russell Thorburn

The Blue Divide
Linda Nemec Foster

Lake, River, Mountain
Mark B. Hamilton

Talking Diamonds
Linda Nemec Foster

Poetic People Power
Tara Bracco (ed.)

The Green Vault Heist
David Salner

There is a Corner of Someplace Else
Camden Michael Jones

Everything Waits
Jonathan Graham

We Are Reckless
Christy Prahl

Always a Body
Molly Fuller

Bowed As If Laden With Snow
Megan Wildhood

Silent Letter
Gail Hanlon

New Wilderness
Jenifer DeBellis

Fulgurite
Catherine Kyle

The Body Is Burden and Delight
Sharon White

Bone Country
Linda Nemec Foster

Not Just the Fire
R.B. Simon

Monarch
Heather Bourbeau

Catch & Release

"Eloquent and gutsy, Lauren Crawford's poems are intimate and unsettling. She writes, 'I am here to survive' as she evidences her resilience while 'pining always for release' and speaking 'death's language.' Her originality is unquestionable. Her poems are infused with untethered energy and art. Few young poets are so gifted and sagacious."

—SUSAN KINSOLVING
National Book Critics Circle Award Finalist
author of *Dailies & Rushes* and *Peripheral Vision*

"From Crawford's opening salvo in which she compares the tracking of a doe in heat to her father whose 'camouflage was… kindness and familiarity' to the poet's closing lines wherein she and her child self-achieve release by becoming a 'trickster in the river, blesser of bodies, / shaper of fissures. Slick as a gill,' *Catch & Release* is a searing revenant to the natural dangers of the world. And the -un. What is natural, I ask, about a father who throws his wife into the fireplace, their child squirming in her crib? What's natural about a mother compelled to hide a daughter's father's suicide until she is of age? What's natural about a poet who grabs you by the hand to lead you 'along the trail of a rapist, a suicide, a criminal' and, despite your forthcomings, you follow? Then, thanks to Crawford, I remember. All of this is natural. The natural that lives in slick and sweat and silence. Natural too and needed is the match light of this collection of visitations. After reading this book, I wanted to resurrect the dead and torture them with their sins. Instead, I clutched my heart. I cried. I reached for the phone and called the ones I love."

—ANDREW MCFADYEN-KETCHUM
Founder & Editor of PoemoftheWeek.com
author of *Fight or Flight* and *Visiting Hours*

"*Catch & Release*, Lauren Crawford's debut collection, is a powerful exploration of memory, and survival. In vivid, unguarded language, she blends the natural world with the inner terrain of trauma—a doe's elusive track, a father's indelible absence, the heat of summer earth, the salt of Gulf waters—all forging a visceral sense of place and presence. *Catch & Release* holds a brutal yet delicate lyricism, asking questions of power, forgiveness, and the hidden music of what lingers. Crawford's poems will pull readers into their stark light, reminding us of the raw beauty in resilience and the strength it takes to hold our past accountable. This is a collection that, once read, will not easily be forgotten."

—JANUARY GILL O'NEIL
author of *Glitter Road*

"'Live the questions now,' Ranier Maria Rilke implores Kappus in *Letters to a Young Poet*, a charge which Lauren Crawford takes up in her gorgeous debut collection of poems, *Catch & Release*. 'How old was I when I / learned to live without a father?,' she asks. In this collection, Crawford expertly steers us through the exquisite infinities of loss, convinced that the sins of any father should not just be resurrected, but held up to the light. This ambitious collection begins 'deep / in cicada country,' where 'Hennessey bottle shards' glimmer the Texas coast, fathers commit suicide and rape, shovelhead sharks knock apple slivers into ocean water, and a speaker emerges from the ash, 'fatherless, / motherless, / loveless, / alive.' If it is true that 'the dead / can sing,' as Crawford suggests, then they sing us toward not just the hallowed ground of personal power, but toward our truest awakenings. This book is an encyclopedia of delight, of survival."

—SARA HENNING
High Plains Book Award Winner
author of *Burn* and *View from True North*

Catch
&
Release

poems

Lauren Crawford

CORNERSTONE PRESS
UNIVERSITY OF WISCONSIN-STEVENS POINT

Cornerstone Press, Stevens Point, Wisconsin 54481
Copyright © 2025 Lauren Crawford

www.uwsp.edu/cornerstone

Printed in the United States of America by
Point Print and Design Studio, Stevens Point, Wisconsin

Library of Congress Control Number: 2025932053
ISBN: 978-1-960329-78-3

Fron cover art by Caleb Linden: https://www.calebtlinden.com/

Cornerstone Press titles are produced in courses and internships offered by the
Department of English at the University of Wisconsin–Stevens Point.

DIRECTOR & PUBLISHER
Dr. Ross K. Tangedal

EXECUTIVE EDITORS
Jeff Snowbarger, Freesia McKee

EDITORIAL DIRECTOR
Brett Hill

SENIOR EDITOR
Ellie Atkinson

PRESS STAFF
Eva Nielsen, Sophie McPherson, Ava Willett, Madison Schultz, Mydasia Zipperer,
Katie Schimke, Abby Paulsen, Reilly Crous, Brianna Loving

CONTENTS

Fatal

After Beth Bachmann

When a doe is in heat, she'll press her back legs together
and piss straight into the spot where her knees meet. Piss
after piss, a black stain grows on the fur like a target or bullet
hole, thick and rank with her scent.

      Desire's punctuation.

The word for the buck that smells her miles away is *hunger*.
By now, it's a blind date with one goal in mind. All the de-
coys and manmade scent markers are no match for nature's
fingerprints.

He knows it's possible someone will get to her before him;
he follows anyway. The muddy hoofprint and blood trail is a
tricky business.

I'll lead you along the trail of a rapist, a suicide, a criminal.

The doe that never pissed: my babysitter.
The hunter in question: my father.

His camouflage was missing the neon, the bright surefire
way to scream *don't shoot*. He was invisible. The usual trap
that everyone knows but no one ever sees coming: kindness
and familiarity.

      The point at the end of a barrel.

When shot, deer don't jump into water to throw off their
scent; they go there so the hunter will never find a body.

Weeding Around Carrots in My Mother's Garden

Kneeling next to my mother in her garden,
our knees marinate in worm manure.
One by one, we pluck carrots like feathers
from loose chicken skin. I wriggle a daisy-gloved
finger beneath the dirt for a plump,
orange scalp and rip it up with a deep, whispery *thump!*
Beside me, my mother dangles each one by the neck
in front of her, shaking the clumps of dirt
that cling between the root hairs.
The only other sound splitting the rhythm
of our harvest is the high-pitched whine
from the dog behind us; the scruff of her neck
clutched in my father's fist shoving her head
down, burying her snout in the loose dirt
surrounding a small, shallow hole she dug
on the other side of my mother's garden.
I steal a glance at her flinging the long,
green stalks onto a growing heap without
turning her head, without saying a word.
Tomorrow, I will eat her steamed carrots
until my plate is empty. And the hole
I see through the window will slowly mud
and pool with rainwater.

Reverse Abuse

Pools of water drag soot into a swirl
up from the shower drain. Each clear droplet
blackens before scaling the slopes

of her calves. Mom scrubs ash into her hair.
When my father comes back home,
his tires wipe clean the dark tracks

on the driveway, he unslams the front door
and hurries inside. As I flail in my crib,
my shrieks slowly lull me back to sleep,

and my mother realizes he's not abusive.
She loves him. My father ungrits his teeth
and pulls Mom out of the fireplace.

He caresses her cheek, cups the pleats
of her frown lines digging into the seams of his
knuckles. He unslaps her and she swallows

the sound of her scream. The chimney inhales
the massive black cloud that surrounds her,
sucking away the smudges on her arms.

My father's spit leaps back onto his tongue
before he swallows it. Mom cooks supper
for us while the chicken unburns on the stove
and the last specks of ash burrow beneath the flames.

Gone

My father wanted to celebrate himself,
so he joined the army and became a medic. God held him
        by the arm and said *Do my work*, hymn chorus
and chapel gong following him to the desert

where his was the last face seen by dying men,
        like the last gospel, as their bodies seeped
into the blood-thickened sand awaiting
        their last morphine drip. They saw him and
screamed their children's names.

He ripped dog tags from the throats of the dead,
        ragged and defeated, and shoved them
into his pockets. If there was no tag, he tugged at chest lapels,
        a loved one's portrait or silver medallions;

anything that marked a dead man for who he was,
        anything that could be etched down
                a logbook labelled K.I.A.

There, on the fields
                that were once date palm orchards
littered with chickpea pods began his pill addiction;
                                death's slow grip.

He watched greasy triatomes drink from severed legs,
        watched their wingbeat cadence, thorax whirl.
He saw death stretch and yawn over the desert
        like a fog, that godawful morning breath.

When he finally fell into a landmine crater,
        ruptured a disk and hollered through the dark oil fire
plumes, the clap of depleted uranium battering the earth
        around him, the deafening shell thud and titanium ricochet,
he spent his first night alone in that pit
        next to a dead brother under the star canopy.

The deep rumble shake beneath his crippled spine,
      his body cradled by war's imprint.
13 hours before reinforcements found him.
        13 hours of moon-white pills from his medicine bag.
        13 hours of bliss in the black.

Lucretia

It was natural for Meg to assume my father was kind; he was.
    That she too would look at his speckled belt, cowboy
boots, his dad bod, even his hair lathered
      in styling wax which smelled like tempered sugar,
      and be comfortable in the plush chair next to him
          in our house while the shadows of their bodies
      shed their whispers to the cracks in the walls,
one of which led to the back door like a pointing finger.

But that night was two glasses of bourbon trickle,
      one bathed in his powdered pills on ice.
          It was blossomless fruit,
             mom working the nightshift,
        me asleep in the other room,
    it was owl wing whistle for the hunt.

Could we have known her haze of their pasture stroll,
      her sight of him blending with cornhusks
          and silver leaf rims as he walked her
             deep into the rows
                of creeping smut?

How did that wind taste?

I can say the deer were passersby,
        I can say the feeder was empty,
      the tickseed buds had yet to open
their jaws, the moss spreading over
      the stone paths waited for no one.
That there was a night cat drinking
      algae trough-water, pawing
          at the circling goldfish with
          nowhere to go.

That no one saw her
      lain in the grass's leaf grit.
      I can say she is still waiting
      for me by the river's mouth,
that she learned a new way to breathe
      under the stars glimmering like streams of dew.
That even now she is looking for me
      above the sleeping cities
between us, higher even than the sound
      of me turning a sun-colored leaf over in my hands.

The day Mom learns my father is a rapist

one cold dusk comes, fall's icy drip,
    and almost at once, the plastic stars
on the walls dim and go out.

In the room next to me, Mom gets a phone call.

    That day, somewhere in the deep woods
        behind our house, a mouse eats its last meal
        where the wild ginger grows thick

and the bare trunks of yew trees mark the height
        of hungry deer with their missing brittle bark.

The shallow tin bucket on the back porch
    clangs all night with rainwater
        and in the morning when the low hill
    mist finally gathers for my mother's
        hum in the kitchen,

    we will have already left that place,
        the sun passing its last yellow
            gleam over the gravel drive,
        and the two horses behind the house
will gallop right through the wire-cut fence.

Graffiti in Nacogdoches, Texas

Outside the hospital, for the first time
the graffiti murals of frowning Natives
follow my mother the second she steps out
into the chill harvest afternoon
               of Nacogdoches.

They sit in rows, heads together,
with pursed painted lips and beaded
foreheads and despite their obvious
disappointment for the vast whites
who now inhabit their land,
               this red-brick town,

to this day they remain a silent reminder of settlement.
The bank, two antique shops, the visitor center
and the bar with a cracked bell above
the door all play host to their faces.

They at once command the passages
through the streets strewn with bluebonnets
and petunia buds. They even direct my mother,
bundled in wool itches, to her car.

Before her last turn by the history museum,
she stops to gaze into the unblinking eyes
of those who first lived here, still frowning
at her for her ancestors' past deeds.

They hold their hands out, palms open
to their onlookers which are far too often
just nesting mockingbirds. But this time,

through the last lights of the day washing
over their plaster braids and peeling cheekbones,
every hand seems to move just where the wall
meets the sidewalk, their fingertips disappearing

beneath the walkways and crossroads
up to the first knuckle, as if each of them
mean to uproot the entire street,
slick with the oils of the day's traffic.

For the first time, my mother sees
their movement and she feels as if
they know who binds her to this place.

They know she waits for escape
and they hear her prayers
collecting in her mouth.

They reach out to her and for longer
than she will ever admit, she lets them
carry her away from the blinks
of a soot-covered world, lets the gusts
of the unknown rewrite her.

Miracle Lemonade

My grandmother, wild with God, digs holes
behind the house where her husband's sins
burrow in the wood planks.
She wears her hair like unclipped shrubs,
                    layered in wilderness.

A small graveyard surrounds her in the forest.
Bare feet in the weeds, she traces letters down
her forearms with the clay stuck to her hands
from her digs. Birds twittle above her. They begin
their stock trades with broomstick straw and garland strings.

Lain before her are the plush toys she took
from my young father and his siblings,
false idols awaiting their final kiss and a thick blanket of red clay.

She baptizes each of them with lemonade and sugar crust,
prays to God to turn the liquid into holy oil before taking a knife
to the blue and pink seams of their chests.
            Then webs of thread loosen in every limb.

She stuffs each one with a quartz crystal before burying them.

Holy heart,
        holy dirt,
                holy finger tracing a cross.

My grandfather's voice whips through the tree line;

                    You out there diggin' again, woman?

Holy wad of hair,
        holy cricket wing,
                holy box with a hole in the lid.

                    That doesn't sound like me, she says.

She's done, heads into the house
to burn more rust in the oven
or serve fruit to the dust mites
like sinners waiting for water,
like God giving out a miracle.

Like Fathers Like Sons

My father, a young boy, sits with his older brother before
the box TV,
        blaring and heavy as a glider missile.

My grandfather thrones the LazyBoy with his youngest child and
only daughter sprawled atop the logs of his lap
        with his hand up her open skirt.

           He lets the pink ruffles tickle his forearm hair.

           My father's questions
      muffle through TV noise.

The word of God is all you need,
his mother repeats if she catches her sons
        peeking anywhere but their Bibles.
           She's unaware of her husband and daughter.

Line by line my father copies the next verse,
in his mind the voice sifting down from the clouds,
             the book of Genesis,

while the neon of a Nerf gun commercial
        flashes across his face,
           swift as a trigger pull.

He awaits the needle sting of his mother's
wooden spoon clap should he recall
the wrong words that once spilled
        from God's lips,
her holler as shrill as a back door slam.
        «»
Long after the parents are asleep,
my father's older brother will slip
        from the folds of his firetruck bedsheets,
           all smoke plume and flannel,

and into the cream twinkle and spring-squeak
        of his sister's bed to play
                    monkey-see, monkey-do,

one paper-thin wall away from my father,
alone in his bed,
        crying and biting a pillow.
He rises and walks into the flickering porchlight gloam,
the sunflower patch across the road
covered in coon tracks.
                This is where I lose my father.

        The swamp bug scuttle,
the flat-bottom boat rotting in the duck pond
muck with bullet holes in the gut outlining
            a faded spray paint target,
        the lapping water speckled with neon BB pellets.

He walks down the road in the middle of the night—
                        he tests his tether.

He leaves the fog-stricken bedroom windows
        and the wind whipping the faded tire-horse swing
            behind him saying
            walk on.

Lightweaver

The first portable camera was introduced in 1685. In-
ventor Nicéphore Niépce used a portable camera obscu-
ra to expose a pewter plate coated with bitumen—also
known as asphalt—to light. He called the process he-
liography which translates to "sun drawing," and this
became the first recorded image.

295 years later, scientists learned how to compress an MRI
machine, install it on a truck, and pull light from the sick on
any given street. Slowly, time shifted the process of filtering
pigments through red-lit

tubs of acetic acid to shock wave units and gamma cameras.
It was light that brought my parents together. Patient after
patient, they wielded light on wheels, like Helios's chariot,
somewhere down the sunlit

hollows of Texas. It's all blots on a screen at the end of the
day. The image of a body cut like a slice of bread, the mag-
net clacking morse code through an open tunnel. A "magnet"
they call the machine that threads light

down labyrinths of ligaments, the maze of the mind, the se-
crets hidden in your bones. Are the vertebra aligned perfectly
like river stones? Are the moons behind the iris still reflecting
a soul's perfect image? Light

that calls the questions down to the blood like a canary. *Where
is the danger?* My father directs the superconductor coils to
hurtle through DNA and diaphragm. *Look to the heart!* My
mother reads the language of light

back to him from the cluttered screen. One day, a mother
that wasn't mine laid down for my father, those bright spears
weaving down her body's hydrogen, sniffing out cerebral ves-
sels for sclerosis. And it was light

he thumbed through her like Apollo's way finder, rooting for the slipped stone in her spine. There, in the dark he finds new land, new charters, new suns. Truth splayed out for him in black and white with nothing but light.

Thunk thunk thunk goes the magnet, *fwisk fwisk fwisk* goes he. Quick as a flash, he mounts her onto the table of his lap, and the images of me, of my mother are fleeing from memory, we are fading away from the light.

Thief

Place me there the night my father let slip he was going to steal me from my mother. Drunk, high, soiled in shame, he counts the days he will be free of his madness, free of a fight he cannot see. He is addicted to pain, and the chemicals it cost to dream his body away. Perhaps he meant to take the horse from our farm and dunk me into a sack, ride all night for the nation's border, hitchhike with immigrants hiding in the semis. Amigo! They sling that spanglish after him, *Vas por el camino equivocado!* Where next, even he does not know. He only knows he wants out, wants me, wants the train to run down the sun. Don't ask me which father I would have chosen; the one who rapes or the one who hits little girls. Ask me which woman I would have liked to become. The one chained to her sorrow, or the one that never would have known a thing.

Self Portrait as a Hippopotamus

In an African folktale, the Creator designed the hippopotamus to live on land in the beginning. For the hippo, something was not quite right; it longed to be in the water and soothe its leathery skin. One day, the hippo asked the Creator to be allowed to live in the water, but the Creator feared the hippo would eat all the water animals with its enormous mouth. An entire ocean in one gulp, if it could. The hippo made a promise to only eat plants and never a single fish. The Creator agreed and granted the hippo permission to live in the water. To this day, hippos spread their dung with their feet to prove to the Creator that there are no traces of fish bones and that they continue to keep the promise their ancestor made.

What message could I smear into the muck
        that says I never fed from the words
               of a good father? Never hashed on a good
        time for a good girl? What can I curl
into the cream of me that hasn't already
        been lost? You can boil my liver and wait
               for the steam to scent you the proof.
        Unstring my inner cords and they'll spell
the secrets of my sadness for you.
        My jaws are wide and I have a vicious snap,
               it's true. But do I not still deserve the taste
        of water when I dream of a sinless father?
I was raised by a predator to be a predator,
        a pup in a wolf's den, the instinct of kill
               and fight nurtured deep within me.
        I'm forever waiting for the absolution
of water. When it rains, I ditch my DNA
        harking me to hunt, and expose my hide
               for the downpour. When we refer to water
        we call it a body. What was that saying
about forgiveness? Something the Christians
        like to say. We come from water,
               we are baptized in water, we are reborn

in water. Angels of rain and shadow,
flick your magic my way and grant me passage
        to the gates of your blessed pools, anoint me
                like your soldiers clad in thunder-darkness.
        Let me feast on something that doesn't cost
the life of another being, the meat
        of another soul. When you're ready to open
                your home, dowse for me with a forked antler
        bone and come find me hiding beneath
all the land dwellers' noses, where I've
        been taught to wait for the kill. Bring me back
                to where I should have been born.

Reverse Metamorphosis

In a dream, Mom, Dad, and I are driving
down a road looking for a hospital. Mom is sick.
As I sit in the waiting room, I glimpse
my father hold up a jar of five live butterflies,
cut mom open with a long, serrated bread
knife, and one by one, he inserts them into
her chest with tweezers. He then looks at me
and places the knife in my hand.

Artichoke 👁

While your curved blooms climb higher,
  the beets rest beneath layers of compost heat,
    eggshell peels, and decaying newspaper headlines
  depicting a stolen girl, a crashed war vessel,
a new vaccine cure-all.

Hard as fists, purpling in the dirt, whether shoved
  in a corner where nothing else will grow or stuck
    between wild catnip, they grow nonetheless.
  Many times, I have wanted to be you, privy
to the prying tongues of bees,

building layers of buttresses inside a thistle shell
  like a cathedral in wartime. At the center:
    your heart; a relic, an alter with holy water,
  a treasure made from sunshine and pure rain trickle.
I, a bloom, a single heart-clutched hand reaching up,

a landmine field around me the color of bruises:
  the beets nursing from the dirt. I, a something to someone.
    I, a word that means people live. I, tempered
  time. I, a scent that says I am ready
to leave, I am ready to see the ordinary,

I am here to survive. I have nothing in common
  with my family with their heads in the ground.
    I am ready to mark myself as different. They find nothing
  from looking up at the sun, why would they?
Up at the distance between us, up at the color

  of sky's undivided attention, up at the hungry eyes of bees,
    up at the benevolent scans of birds searching for seed
  while I build my temple that tastes like sugar
at least to someone; while I open my mouth to drink.

The Day My Father Dies

I.

On the last day of deer season my mother,
losing daylight for the hike back home, lets the buck
in her sights browse for the last kernels of corn
scattered under the feeder before strolling on without ever lifting
his head, perhaps not even after she lowers the barrel of her
gun, lets it thud on the cold rigid carpet beside her boots and
leaves the deer blind, letting the wood-split door clap behind her.
She'll keep it loaded on her walk back, flinching when she
hears rabbits snap twigs and bats stretching their wings.

II.

She won't tell me my father has shot himself
until I turn eighteen. She won't trip over the ores
of speckled granite jutting out from the hills,
nor the spiked palms of prickly pear, their purple prune
thumbs once lining the edges already fallen and burst,
bleeding shriveled in the crabgrass weeds. Past that ragged
oak gate with the rusted hinge and the cattle beams
on which the horses scratch their rumps, she'll reach me
at the cabin keeping warm between the folds
of my sleeping bag next to the wood burning stove.

III.

Before she steps through the door, one hand on the knob,
night's gloom will fight to bathe her against the weak
porchlight blinking at the moth swarms. She'll dream of a shot
ten-point at the bottom of a pond, having given up the hunter's
chase for a mouthful of water. Come summer when
the shoreline slinks back, his antlers will poke through the surface
like a hand reaching up for air, like a cry no one will hear;
its reflection bracing for a fall that will last forever.

On My Father's Suicide

East Texas, 2011

This piece of land looks like a scab and the tall
weeds bow towards me while I crunch along.
The air cottoning my mouth tastes like
gunpowder and gasoline. Now deep
in cicada country, their gradual crescendo
and decrescendo sounds like the breaths that
come before sleep, like a rain that never quiets.
When I reach the clearing where he used to live,
a vulture loiters on a dying tree beside it, staring
at me approaching him. I wonder if this bird,
hunched and tired, saw my father die in this place.
How long did he watch my father kneel here in this
yard, teeth clamped on the gun's barrel, before he
lurched, alone, a distant rumbling in the open sky;
the only witness of his passing? Did the ground
shrug with relief, grateful for my father's quick
untethering? A lit match, certainly no one
can see from space, going out.

Smoke

I dreamt my father scribbled his suicide
        note on cigarette paper, & for the filling,
he rolled my hair like dry weed, cinched

tight in a thin coat of tissue. When he lit
        the tip, the glow from the cig, golden as suns, haloed
his puckered mouth as night's dark

curtain opened for him. He stood alone in a field beneath a
        sky redacted
of its moon and stars, silent save for the creak

of his boots on husk and stone. The smolders climbed closer
        to his lips, eating the words
he wrote, and the ashes scampered away

from him as if they meant to hide in the dewing grass. With
        each plume of breath, I saw him
practice his release, his letting go. He threw

the spent cig when he was done, its spit-soaked seams curled
        around the frayed knot of my hair
I imagined he hitched onto night's

ether, asking simply to drive on.

Galveston

That Houstonian swamp, intimate with the gulf
and her cries, shurling and foamy, the pocket beds
of seaweed peppered with July picnic garlands

and hollow firework shells, Hennessey bottle shards
that gleam brighter than nail polish glaze. They stud
the beach that I, so many, many times, have chosen

as an escape from pitiful fights with my parents
or lying boys, or even my own depression, hollering
at gulls nipping at perch gills braided with bright fishing

twine, each bloody seam opened wide like a hand fan.
There was the gleaned shore, hours before sunrise, its spoils
of the night—toothed conches and whole gritty sand dollars—

stowed fresh on every tourist shelf of the bay in neat rows
all labeled ocean novelty. There was my collection of oyster
shells pre-shucked by the wide veins of jetty parting

the major port like long, sharp fingers stretching
into the gulf, waiting to shake hands with the ocean.
There was the warm prickle of sea spray behind my knees

and the rip current tumble dirtying my hair after a plunge.
I want the pink and orange sky nestled atop the sun
and bay like settled wine tannins. I want the sheer mist

of gulf roils lain on me like a mother's dense kiss.
Sinful reams of starlight rooting me in the sandshift;
the Atlantic's everchanging nook. Give me the pelicans

sunning on rotting dock posts infested with algae, waiting
for the skittish minnows to ripple the surface. Give me
the open dark water ready to ambush oil rigs or breed

hurricanes the shape of bad secrets. Give me waves
the color of age itself, let me gulp the salt-stained air
after I've carved my name again into the crumbling deck

rail of the wharf like I own the ceaseless swell of barnacle
teeth and mullet leap, like I could look at the foaming
lips closing over the gannets diving for shrimp knowing

that even if I swallowed the world whole in one massive gulp,
offer my open throat, I would still be starving for more.

The Mullet Leap 👁

The mullet fish, or grey mullet, is most known for its two distinguishing leaps. The first, a straight clear dart out of the water, no higher than a foot or two, helps them escape predators. The second leap, the slower, lower jump with a twirl to the side, is mysterious. The fish takes his time with it, like drawing a hash mark in the air with incredible accuracy, one sheen scale brightening neatly after another. The first time I saw it, questions bubbled in me. Why that elegant, unrushed leap? Was it all simply a dance? Something the fish wanted to show off? Was it an announcement that life exists somewhere we do not? The little girl in me once thought the mullet secretly worshiped the land-dwellers, and that long, second leap was their baptism; the same as ours when we go to the river to pray and bathe in the psalmy water. Perhaps, drenched in praise and glory, he means to show it all off: that holy double dorsal, the pharynx engorged in absolution, the dagger-shaped lips swollen pink like a lover's. Maybe he goes belly up begging for a kiss from the gods of the green. Maybe the mullet is like me: wanting for a realm it can never have, a heaven seemingly only a leap away. Alone, I can hear him praying for the sky god's favor, praying with me. Kiss me, he taunts. *Kiss me. I dare you.*

Burial

It's fall in the garden and the leaves on the basil freckle
with black. I am thinking of the signs of my father

dying. It's easy enough to see in my plants; the cilantro,
albeit cold-clever, eventually blossoms with seed

one crisp January morning. Its leaves, like a diseased
heart, grow smaller and smaller, duller and duller

until it can do nothing but shove the white flowers,
tiny as a pin, up to the sky in clear, utter surrender.

I'm ready to die, they all seem to say. Here is my father
in the kitchen, bent over the sink, his guts spewing

from his gills. Later he sips tea and loses the strength
to hold up a hardback. Slurs siphon his tongue,

like the ones I serenade to the moon slinking
the salamanders to sleep. I know how to lull down

the clematis before she stutters into winter's
submission. I speak death's language like a land lark

to my bloomers at bedtime. At my tender words,
chloroplast will quicken, water quitting cytoplasm

for the safety of the roots, and any remaining sap
unbraids from vacuole, sweet resin of the gods,

and slowly rebrands as antifreeze. But father?
When did your ribosomes rupture? Where did you

begin unshackling the dregs of your breath? When did
you start hating your life? Mine? Ours? Where were all

your mitochondria when you decided to leave me, your
only daughter? Where was your glucose, your sisters

of sugar, when I needed you? I understand my mother
was not green at the time, none of us were.

I, too young, and she a season too late. Maybe she
balmed your lips with honey when she saw your end

looming. A husband and another daughter later,
she cultivated her green thumb as an insurance policy.

Never again, she promised herself every night after you
died. To this day, and every year, her tomatoes are

shockingly bulbous, her figs flourish under her careful
tutelage, and her grapefruit tree towers so tall it lilts

over the neighbors' fence, fruit promisingly sour and
succulent. It's all so beautiful and heavy, a mother's

clear proof that she will never let her family die again.
You were there, I somehow knew it, the year she

began transcribing the delphinium's dialect to me,
the lupine's lingo. Now, deciphering death is as easy as

instinct, at the cost of all the things you went without:
cover, warmth, light, love.

The Music in Silence 👁

Music is the silence between the notes
—Claude Debussy

If silence is rest and rest is music, then the dead
          can sing and the song I hear from that quiet cemetery
belongs to my dead father singing like a cowboy
        whose voice corrals between mountain tops.

He sings like an animal who will never find
        a mate. In the morning, he sings like the hum
of dragonflies who putter the cattails as if
        they were keys on a piano. He sings

like nothing is his. He sings like windstreams
        whistling through the arms of river gum trees
bearded with Spanish moss. The chord
        rattles their trunks, shooing the screech

owls from their roosts. The rain is his conductor.
        He sings like a brook that will never dry up
or clog with duckweed slush. He plays
        the bulrush reeds as if they were chimes.

His deep slow trill sifts through the fog like silt
        through a net. He sings like a blind night bird.
He sings like the valley behind him is his flute.
        He funnels the open sky for air so he'll never

once need to pause for breath. I hear him now beneath
        my feet while I cover his grave with hay, shushing
his tune. Still, it drags me home like a sail that will
        never find land, like a string with me tied to the end.

The Taste of Loss

Father, I think of you at harvest time in my garden,
        clugging in my boots to the foot of the raised
cabbage bed, blade in hand, severing the plump green
        heads and chucking them in a basket.

I think of you in the first house
        we lived in with the brush-thick
field and the finch-feathered lemon trees.
        There's a clatter of something
metal in the background, the bickering
        crow's claws on the tin roof,

There's a plate of food untouched where you sit,
        next to the pile of cigarette ash forming
the star you trace with your finger.

        How easily you lied to yourself about the
hilltops you thought you'd never hike, how easily you
        named the sun for the things it, too, touched;
you, the paddleboats and the lake and the sand beds
        embroidered with shark teeth.

The last thought before you fell asleep at night
        was always how hungry you were.
Far too soon you tasted the rush of trespass.
        Far too soon you lost me

the way the moon loses the night for the golden slits
        of daybreak and the hellbent breaths of the
living. I listen for the warblers trying to sneak
        a quick blueberry in the bushes behind

my back while I fiddle with the leafy collars
        on the cabbage heads, knowing even
if I catch them in the act, they can all still flee.

Pillars of Salt, Pillars of Ghosts

I.

Allah, God, Gabriel, and the prophets have all agreed,
after convalescing on a sunspot, that Sodom, deviants of sex,
Gomorrah, slaves of sin, must burn. They are all fated
to be rendered down, feasted by Gaia's wormy mouth.
Little lady married to Lot, sliver of salt, the men of your time
have deemed you too curious for your own skin. Your hands
are slick with the pleasures of the earth. When angels
of the oversouls gave you a chance to leave and lead
toward righteousness, they warned: *Look back and become*
earth again. Look back and don a ghost's gear. Look back,
and smell death's black breath. Why did you look back?
Was it because your home was burning? Did you love
your people even though you knew they couldn't be saved?
You saw the naked hands of The Creator, heaving down
consequence like a Hammer of Sol. What did you see
when you looked into the eye of a sunbreaker? Your name
precludes you, Ada or Edith, the prophets did not bother
writing you down when they decided to show their people
the result of disobedience. But only you have seen
the Bearer of Light when you dared look back at all
you ever knew; where cleansing flames dined on half
of your heart. Now, your blood feeds the cicadas nesting
dormant in the crooks of a dead goddess's body. Your calves
are licked clean by the oryx and the mongoose in winter.
Whisperer of the Worm, what secrets had Gaia been sharing
with you on the day you shivered into a pillar of salt?
Did she know something the man's god did not? About love?
About darkness? About regret? Your mistakes are etched
into the seams of your stone mouth. Your dreams are crowded
with Titans, sired glorious by the Lady who cradles you
now in the dust. You are still incandescent after a thousand
or two years in the sun, forever stilled by unforgiving gods.

II.

The day after I lost my mother,
I went to see my best friend, Christina, in New York City.
She had purchased a birthday ticket to see *Hadestown*
on Broadway. It was already sold out by the time I got there,
so she had to go without me. All day before the show,
she eulogized every number of that musical.

Wait for me, I'm coming, too, she trilled to me the voices
of every Greek god who advised Orpheus, Son of Song,
to rescue his love, Eurydice, from the underworld.
In the Barnes and Noble, uncaring who heard or saw
my unabashed smile there was her gorgeous adagio
gifted to the concrete peasants of her kingdom,
                                    the pigeons pecking in the gutter.

All the way down to Chinatown. Here come the Fates flocking us:

    Where do you think you're going? Who do you think you are?

We double back to Brooklyn when we lose the subway to a train
conductors' strike. Money is too tight in this town for the trailblazers
of the track. This night, no one lights our way.

    The River Styx, like the Hudson, is wide
    with walls of iron, lined with wire and reams of dying dreams.

Closer now, Hermes and my girl guides us to the gates of the underworld:
Times Square, five stories of Macy's, and the Public Library
housing the voices of the dead and the lion heads
wrestling out a roar to the wayward stranger. The belly of Broadway
opens for Christina, a nymph in pink,
                                    lips lacquered,
                                            lashes inked black.

I'm going to cry, she tells me before she chases
after Orpheus and his foolishness.

Ticketless and alone, my girl gone to gamble with Hades,
I sneak around to a stilted window and peer through the panes
like an oracle.

Hades asks his children who is the enemy
and the company says it's poverty. They want
what they can't have and that's reason enough, it seems,
to build an infinite wall of stone and malice. Eurydice
traded her empty belly for a new home gilded in ghosts.

This is a story of how a man and his song budged Fate,
tumbled walls,
moved the gods.

A song, Orpheus gave to the train tracks
    when no cars would carry him down.
A song, he used to make the wallstones of Hadestown weep,
A song, he plucked from the tongues of the Fates:
Say I do, he knelt before Eurydice with nothing
but a flower in his hands. A song, he pleaded
to Lady Persephone, when he heard of the leash,
the contract, the deal chaining his lover to the dead.

And the dead, she can blink away, Lady of the Unliving,
as easy as falling leaves. But the love of Orpheus,
strong and unflinching as Heracles' brow,
culled the tendons of the Lady's heart, which we all know,
is tender and fragrant as Spring.

A new deal, new cards, a new challenge, a test for Hermes
to deliver in the name of love. It's dark and late outside
in New York, but Orpheus has done well so far.

Hades, Eurydice, the Dead, Persephone.

*If your love for her is pure, you should have no problem
proving it, says the Grey Lord.*

We all watch the two lovers jostle skittishly up the road
to the living in single file. Christina, sister of Clotho,
already mourns Orpheus's loss in dark, thick streams of salt.
She, unlike me, knows his destiny. As does Hades,
the flawless gambler. One second of doubt, one speck
of suspicion, one look back at Eurydice, and The Rich One
can yank her back down to hell. Back he will snatch
her soul for his legion of sycophants.

Say it's not true, I plead with the Fates, with Christina's teary scowl.

Man and woman of the earth, you are listened and loved
by a crowd thousands of years ahead of the darkness.
As far as you, Orpheus, think you lie between victory and death,
a life with your lady if only you had not a shred of doubt
you were doing the right thing, you were with the right
woman, you were fighting the right fight.

Doubt, the saying goes, is the true enemy, the liar,
the unforgiving. Not Hades, not death, not hell, not hate.

Doubt untwists love from lover, unbinds the brave from the broken,
unkinks the committed from the damned. And damned I am in the
streets,
fatherless,
motherless,
loveless,
alive.

III.

I'm heading into the depths of hell to retrieve you, father.
Step after step, I know the dangers of this place. Boiled brass,
coiled hate, suffering unstoppered. Questions surround me
like light in a dark tunnel. Where am I going to find you?

Another step, more danger, demons lurking in a palace of brass.
You are named after a king, a slayer of Goliath. Where is your
light at the end of the tunnel? Am I going to find you
chained to a slab of darkness? Or smoking somewhere in an oven?

You serve a new king that no god, no Goliath can slay in your name.
Satan was once an angel, a harbinger of safety and saints.
He, too, was chained by slabs of darkness. Like you, He smoked sin,
hurt the innocent, He defied the rules of love.

Satan, angels, harbingers of saints, what will happen if I look back
when I save my father from hell? Do you forbid it? I'm already here
and I don't know why. He hurt the innocent. He betrayed the rules of love.
What will I see if I turn my cheek to you? Will my body return to salt?

Father, I'm saving you from this hell you've lived. It's forbidden, but I'm ready
to face you again. I have my questions here in a pile on my shoulders;
little burdens burning holes in my cheeks. Why did you salt a body
that wasn't yours? Why did you leave me? I can't see you yet, it's dark

down here. Face me again and hear my questions pile up like the dead.
Will you follow me if given the chance to be good? Do you hunger
for the dark, still, or do you want to leave with me? This is my biggest fear.
I battle the black, I save a sinner, I reach for you, and you still

might not take my hand. Are my chances even good? Follow me,
father, please. I'm filling with hate; the devil sees me. Place me back into
the cage of your heart, where I can battle out the black, clean sins
like water in a Father's hand. Quick, to the stairs, don't look back

at the devil who hates seeing his souls fleeing his palace. Don't
wait for the sound of his howl, like night lashing at our backs, the
whip as quick as a father's hands. You're behind me, I don't need to look
to know you're there. I'm heading out of the depths of hell with my father.

Exile

It's the winding road I remember,
        the young pine trees given over
to the wisteria vines,
        a thousand purple blooms,
their breath sweet and sharp
        like an Old Fashioned nestled
around a single cube of ice
        laced with sugar swirl. The rock
stream guttering into the pasture after
        a good rain. There were two horses
with funny names on that piece
        of land, the bay and the black,
gated by the blackberry thorn fence,
        their canes that shot between the wire.
How many summers did I comb
        down the line with the bay licking
the back of my neck, snorting in my ear?
        How many bucketfulls did I present
to my mother with bloody fingers
        dyed purple? How old was I when
I learned to live without a father?
        How many times did I chase kittens
behind the house with melting
        Twinkies in my hands for bait?
How hard did my mother swat them
        for shredding the loaves of
bread after I begged her to let them
        wild and loose into the house?
I can see them all clearly now,
        white paws high tailing through
the door, the shape of them,
        like tiny nimble ghosts, disappearing
beneath the giant magnolia tree
        blooming white in the sun just
beyond the fence line. They are
        blowing right past the kibble tins,
they are leaving me for good.

Mother and Me, Alone

August in Texas and Mom cuts off an old man staring
at the dried apricots in the middle of the lane,
the wheels of the cart screech in her maneuver,
almost as if to dignify it and I sense that if the bagged
fruit had eyes, they'd be glaring too. Our canned
peaches and almond granola shift and clatter
when we shuffle right into our nosy neighbor, Hal,
at the end of the lane. He's fluent in neighborhood
crime, checking the "Next Door" Facebook group
by the hour for an update on whether the town will finally
prohibit the homeless from chaining their dogs up in the woods
while they loiter beneath the hefty overpass bridges
in the heat begging for their next meal. He demands the animals'
rescue; *it's just inhumane*, he says. I hurry for the next
free sample dome behind him, and pluck a glossy
sugared fig from the papered sack resting
on the stand and suck on the dark pulp as I browse
through the floral section, pinching the head
of a crisp yellow daisy when I think no one's
watching and tucking it away in my pocket. I drift
farther away from my mother beyond the algae tanks
full of guppies bubbling in their own
language, and soon enough I imagine my dead father
bleachered on a broad row in the store, his lane
labeled clearance. He mouths the word *father* at me,
and like a child choosing a toy, I wonder if I want one.

Flower Girl

New father at the end of this carpeted trench,
below the bell gongs and organ shrill,
I see you like a green light without a map,
an endless road stretching before me, mud-
slick and weed crowded. Your eyes are
unexplored land. You look at me, careful
sparrow, in hawk territory, wing thrash
looming. You stand on the harsh
marble steps, reflective in their gloss polish.

When it's over, you kneel beside me
at the altar, your vows to love me and my
mother hang in the air still dense as morning
mist. The photographers beg me to kiss
your cheek for a picture, hug your neck, your
aftershave spice, place you there in my heart
where someone once was like a new pair of shoes
that'll never quite fit. My lips meet your skin

like braille to a finger when you pretend
to pout, my new grandmother cooing me from
behind the camera with *Come on sweetie, just once
for the picture.* When I follow you and my mother
out of that church to greet our new family,
In my mind I move down the aisle
like a drowning gull flailing against a shore
worn smooth by a ceaseless lake wind.

Golden Shovel

After Beth Bachmann

No matter how much I desire it, a

                    car ride will always turn a bruise lilac.

I finger the little sebum deaths of my cheek where my new
father struck me. Can

I braise in the back seat next to my sister glowing in her
innocence? The little peach. Hold,

I say to myself and the lint dust twirling between my
thumbs. Hold on

to the wilting trilliums you picked from the last rest stop.
They lie half-dead

in my lap where I simmer in my own salt. I try to catch my
mother's face. Is she green for

it? The car turns toward home, reduced from 85 mph, and
the flowers will drink for days.

Ode to the Rabbit Call

There is no sound in the world like a distressed rabbit call.
Some will say it's different for everyone who hears it.

Some think it's the sound of a rusty Ford hood slamming shut
or the last wail of a cat birthing kittens. *Is it over yet? Tell me*

this is the end, she thinks. But no one knows this sound better than
teenage me getting caught red-handed stirring up mischief.

A million different Southern-style punishments whiz through
my mind within milliseconds, each more horrifying than the next,

and not knowing which it will be. Not knowing the day, the time,
the second, the memory of my own release. That sound,

that scream, was the noise my window made when I snuck out
as a teen to meet some boy across the neighborhood pond,

and waited to greet me on my return. It was the creak of the
third-to-last stair leading to the rooms where my family slept,

and the final whistle of my door wheezing shut. The rabbit's call,
the sounds of my childhood home, even my mischief brewing

a mile down the road share the same message: *I will die
if I am caught*. To the hunter, it sounds like dinner. Oil bubbling,

fat making that quick shushing sound, the kind they tended
to angle at me. I imagine it is worse for the rabbit in the colder

months. Within a matter of weeks, the rabbit must relearn how
to alter her own pigment to blend in with the snow. Her instincts

for survival are also changing; she must now account for hunting
season, and every god forsaken thing she does makes more noise

than it did before. Every move, every goal is an equation now.
Each step must be measured for its energy, its damage, its deadly

noise. Snow crunches underfoot, rocks tumble in an amplifying
mess down a hill, and sound carries further in the cold to all

the wrong ears in the world. I have shared the rabbit's illogical
paranoia. I feared that somehow my folks could hear my

footsteps from a neighborhood away. Could hear the iron gates
of a loverboy's home swinging its arms wide open for me.

Could even hear my mouth curling wickedly into a smile
the second I captured something for myself at last; a moment,

a thought, a free gaze at the dark, glittering sky. There is no
sound in the world like that. There is no dash, no clean shot

through a bush or under a fence that will save you once within
the sights of a dark figure, fifty yards out, holding your fate

in their hands. A mountain of pleasure in an instant,
                              killed by the shuck of a bullet.

Things I Inherited from My Father, According to a Mother Before Her Glass of Wine

After Jennifer Espinoza

Being neurodivergent, and not knowing. Being a girl,
but not wanting to be a girl. Being angry, using bad
words, bad looks, bad posture, bad habits.

Keeping bad company as my only friend; the girl
down the street who steals cigarettes from her mom
and kisses me behind the Walgreens.

Interrupting people because I'm afraid I'll forget
what I wanted to say by the time someone is finished
speaking. Having my own thoughts.

Forgetting the names of streets I have been down
when I am taking my driver's test, when I am looking
for a coffee shop. Wanting to be alone.

Not talking. Talking. *You're selfish*, she tells me.
How dare I speak my mind when I disagree.
How dare I call down the leaves like a witch

and wrap myself in dust before bed. How dare I spell
the sun away from her house plants, her darling
daughters. How dare I purchase string undies

from the store against step-sir's wishes. How dare I
dress like a whore. I bring pants when asked to wear
a dress and I am disrespectful. I wear a dress

when asked to be professional and I'm a tramp.
I asked her one time how to be a good woman
and she told me to be obedient, be flexible with

your man like water. *But water is not flexible when it gets too hot or too cold*, I wanted to tell her. And I am always too hot or too cold, too something, too

everything. Just like you. Just like father. Just like nothing.

Present Day Connecticut

I visit a better version of my mother in my dreams.
We're high, and she looks out the window
of the living room to complain about snowfall.
There's no reason for it, but she calls the climate crisis
a beast dappled in spun sugar. I fill her mug
with nettle straw and shriveled huckleberries
beyond the proper ratio to boiling water,
beyond the proper ratio to anything she's ever given me.
Outside a truck driver mimes at a car as it slows
right into the rinds of the highway rails sloped with sheet ice.
NBC Connecticut News tells me there was a 1.4 magnitude
earthquake this afternoon, but I might not have felt it.

What I Have in Common with a Shovelhead Shark

We're on the bay boat, thirty miles deep into the Gulf
of Mexico. I've got a shark that's too big for my pole
on the line. It takes forty-five minutes to reel it in.

When the line gets too rough, step-sir takes over and
gives my arms a break. This is a fight with a creature
we don't yet know. But somehow, he knows.

Before his long, amber tail flicks a little too close to the
surface, before that pointed nose thrashes through the
water, he somehow knows what I've got. My arms ache,

my sun-stained forehead sweats, and I'm out of breath
trying to rip my prize from its home, from everything it
knows. Soon enough though, the fight is over, we win,

and all five massive feet of the shark is in the boat with
us, razor teeth slashing, that wicked tail wreaking havoc,
knocking lures, bobbers, and apple slivers overboard.

I back away, not knowing what to do, but sir rushes
forward and begins bashing that shovelhead with his
fist, right between the eyes. *I have to knock him out,*

he says, *or he'll hurt someone when we try to handle
him.* Bang goes sir's fist: bang, bang, bang. It takes
a while, the shark is strong, but for once, I am grateful

for his violence. For once, its function is truly protection.
Each blow slows the shark's stuttering movements until
his knuckles begin to bleed. For once, we all agree it's

necessary and I can't stop looking. Those dorsal veins
popping, the swift and elegant force of his swings.
How brutally beautiful it must be to kill a king.

When it's over, sir's hand is wrecked. *Out of water,*
their skin is like sandpaper, he tells me, *feel him.*
And I do. I run my hands along my catch,

down that long, golden body leaking the Gulf from his
gills. In my mind I try to piece together where I belong,
how I am meant to live but all I can hear is that stiff,

hollow sound, that bang rattling the boat like a signal,
like I'm simply waiting for something to end.

How It Feels to Lose Someone

Like a splinter so thin I can't see it
Slipping between my grip
Over and over I run my finger
Across my skin to check if you're still there
Like a groomer searching for ticks
Or a wasp stinger lodged in a child's thigh
After giving up for some time
I'll forget until I sit on a stool
At just the right spot
And there you are
Yet again I cannot resist
Yet again I drag my finger
Across my skin looking
For you
Looking
Everywhere.

Anvil

My dentist speaks calm and silvery
to the center of my open mouth.

You will need a few crowns on these worn down teeth.
He barbs at my lower jaw with tools
made slick by my own spit.

Do you grind your jaw at night? Yes, I grind
my jaw at night. Since I was a girl,
actually.

Are you stressed? My gums seem to be
whispering to him. He's learned to nose
out answers where they lay.

Again, he waits for pain to make its
work on my face. The tools slither
between my lips, but I know not to bite.

I feel the answers in me,
lapping at my cheeks like saltwater.

The color of abuse is an empty root
canal, an endless night of tooth grapple;

little anvils of light clashing in the dark;
my tongue forever caught in my throat.

Poem to the Unnameable Father

I have finally caught you on my line. I'm still young,
we have years to go once you're in the boat with me,
once I've convinced you how to breathe, how to shed
your scales and grow legs, how to skate on ice and

hold my hand. For a time, I know you'll not
understand why I've taken you. I won't say I'm sorry
I pilfered you from wherever you were before.
Had you another wife? Another daughter? A job you

liked? Somehow, I think it was oil rigs, or perhaps
piracy. I know how you love the sea, but I want my
father. We'll fight at times, like we are now; you on
the hook, me clutching the reel. I'll hold you gingerly

in my hands while I wrestle the hook from your lips,
smeared with my bait; the thin shreds of a lonely girl's
heart. Please don't smack my hands with your tail,
please don't twitch toward the water. When we get

home, you'll begin to learn again how to be a father
and this time, it'll work. Lord knows how long
I've tried to catch you, the lengths I have gone.
I sang for you on the rocks of the jetty. I chummed

the water with warm laughter. At midnight, one time,
I stole a can of tobacco from the Seven Eleven
and dunked it into the tidepools where I saw you
finning the water. I kept a pinch, chewed, and spat

as far as I could. I dug sand pits, flung chicken thighs
soaked in sugar and beer at the waves. I laid crab
traps lined with my old baby pictures. I even casted
with your old Beatles cassette on my hook. I got close

that time, I heard a low sound lifting through
the water. It sounded like a fence falling down in
a field, like a sigh, like twigs unspooling from a nest.
A little like me, even. Like you were never really gone.

Let Set for 5–10 Minutes

I spilled ink
on the part
of my poem
where I said
how much I
loved you.
It was a beautiful
note, I wrote
it between
scenes of the movie
I was watching
with my clay mask
still on my face. I
couldn't move a single
muscle to smile, so
I figured
I'd write it
down. After I spilled
the ink, I rewound
the movie
and watched
the scenes I missed,
then washed my face clean.

Ode to my Blank Page

You ask nothing of me, watchful bystander.
You have my secrets. You know when a good
idea is near, even when I don't.

You know my darkest shame: rape and pedophilia
        have infested my family tree.
You keep me up late, and we watch night
        tell its tales through my window. Mosquito dinner,
a luna moth caught in a hailstorm,
        the road armadillo picked clean.
            Starling arpeggio.

Am I me when I am alone with you?

While I hold my past accountable
        you make a crawl space out of moonlight,
            not nearly large enough for my insomnia's sake.

I am constantly looking to glean sifted afterlight
        from the keyboard, knock out
a pattern of clicks like cricket dance,
        one that carries a tune long
after it's done and gone.
            Deep vibrato.

You hold a tuning fork next to my work
like a black light; invite me to improve.
            Adjust.

I use you to conduct music for others,
        but mostly for myself. You are my stage,
my chessboard, my violin,
        my "Do Not Disturb" sign.
When you tell me to write poetry,
        I hear strings and winds, loaded rest;
an orchestra beyond words or metaphor;
        all I have to make people listen.

Say Her Name

Say her name.
>   *Meg*, when I have forgotten your face,
>>   plain and ordinary to everyone but me,
>   when I forget the freckles that form
>   a triangle on your cheek, forget
>   the dirty sand tint of your hair,
>>   your grin full of scattered teeth.

Say her name.
>   *Meg*, when I can't remember the first time
>>   I saw you smoke, when I lose the shape
>   of the back of your head in your beat up Kia,
>   my car seat squirms, your cigarette puffs
>   streaming in the dust we leave pluming
>   behind us, your two-fingered shake at me
>>   *Don't tell Nana*,
>>   breathe and shed the ash,
>>>   breathe and shed the ash.

Say her name.
>   *Meg*, come to me as if my father had never forced
>>   you beneath him, possibly in my place
>   had you refused, had you run, had you bent
>>   the crossbeams of the roof with your recoil.

Say her name.
>   *Meg*, come to me when you can bear
>>   to look at my face and not see danger.

Say her name.
>   *Meg*, come to me when I am offshoot foliage.
>>   Walk me down a peony trail and release me
>>   from my dead father's grip, from broken
>>   beanrunner bine and leaflitter filth.

Say her name.
>   *Meg*, come to me when you are sweet orange peels,
>>   foxglove horns eager for bumblebee fuzz,
>>   the nectar bounty of a dozen clover poms. Give me
>   your hurt and I will wash it clean.

Say her name.
    Meg, come to me when you can ease
        through darkness like the stretching
        arms of ivy, comfortable and blind,
      without the moon's beacon;
       when you are your own luster,
        when you are earthshine.
Say her name.
    Meg, believe me when I say you have become wind,
      the last breath of sundown spilling
        sideways across hemlock hills.
   You lift into the day, as wind will, into the fold
    that is the earth's curves, guide the leaves,
    red and crisp, in their last tumble,
     speak whistle-tongue,
      and feel all the birds fly.

Cowcatcher

A man that looks like my father walks past me where I sit on a bench
in the park where pigeons peck the flesh off tossed peach hearts.
A train screams, he scuffs on and the dogs keep running.

In this courtyard, the homeless breathe their dreams through
harmonicas; a tune that can keep their fingers warm in the wind
where a man walks by me, looks for the fountain to toss his change,

the lint clung to the silver face of a father. When it rains the coins
sleep under the trickle, the overflow, the tarps pooling with water
while the train screams a warning and goes on scuffing the tracks;

it will not stop here. Winter's come and the homeless follow rabbit
treads in the snow; another meal, another kill, another book with
a pen in my lap. *That's not you*, I say when a father walks past me

to his pickup, his dog leaping out of the frost for the backseat.
He dirties the seams with his cold nose. Together they leave for home,
far away from the police siren screams, the train horn; the lowest

chord of distance breathing through the trees. It's Christmas yet,
and again I flip another page on this park bench. I was a girl
when my father walked away from me in a town where
the train never stops screaming and he never stops running.

What I Would Pack in a Bento Box
for the Little Girl Version of Me

i.

A salve I have made from stars and sundance,
to soothe the words you are not ready for.

The ones that are thrown all too carelessly
down the stairwells of your school, your home,
your work, and later your own mind.

Whore. Freak. Bitch. In those moments you will
need to learn how to gather light by yourself.

ii.

I know you have a stash of hearts hidden somewhere
       behind the shelves of the school

library. Between volumes twelve and thirteen
       of the Britannica Encyclopedias

where no one cares to look. Let me tell you
       I understand your wants; to love and be

loved as badly as breathing. We both know whose hearts
       they are and for what purpose

you hoard them. I would give you my own again
       and again, my chest pried open like a clam

and scraped clean for you, but it cannot be done.
       The next time you visit your hearts,

you'll need to feed them. I'm packing a fuck for them,
       the only thing they can survive on at

    this point.

iii.

A single sheet of dried seaweed for the wayward secrets
you pickpocket from the concrete. Wrap them in this,
like you did the hearts, and sling them up a flagpole,
safely away from the leering ears of the land-dwellers.

iv.

A list of sorrys for you to hand out.
            You have your moments,
you fling words of your own
            before you've weighed them
like an eel with a tail of lightning.
            But you do not know who takes
your stings. Blind is your aim.
            I have the names already
taken down for you. I know
            what they plan to say tomorrow
and the next day and the next.
            You are so easily drawn, shot
and cut off by the right strike of teeth.
            We'll mourn your tail once it's taken,
mourn the things you bit back.
            I know what threatens to drown you.
Your gills are bruised, your jaws have worn
            down from grinding, but you are not
going to die in this place.

v.

Fresh beluga caviar (your favorite). A delicacy that
befits your station in the food chain. The first and only
time we ever tasted this was by chance, theft, and luck.

The most popular girl in sixth grade had hunkered all
day over an obscene cake, secretly baked for us as an
apology for the Gymnastic Birthday Fiasco of '07.

Her extravagant mother had forced her to invite us for an
actual pity party; an absolution of the girlhood faith.
That night, we slumbered under the pink and white silks

of that girl's privileged life like blessed princesses.
When you and I snuck into her fam's fridge in that
colossal steel kitchen, it was by chance those inky,

black pearly dears were there, stacked neatly in their
cases like a thousand little pupils shucked clean from
their iris. It was by theft we indulged the true flavor

of the sea, of another world entire. And it was by luck
that when each globe shivered its way to our soul,
no one woke from the tiny screams of all that life

skittering across the tongue. How beautiful a thing like
that was. An overabundance of life, just for you,
produced in anticipation of violence.

vi.

If the math teacher tells you to change your clothes again,
remember the lemon I have packed for you. The one
that smells like him if left out in the sun too long.

You're in the south, remember? Not everyone was born
with honey in their mouth and a genuine prayer on their lips
as their god has commanded of them. They're more likely

to see a bra strap and hope for acid rain; for the air and water
around us to be as nasty and poisonous as them. They don't know
you've been microdosing pain since your father died.

They have no idea that sour is your favorite flavor. They don't
know how to measure the proper dosage of misogyny
for a young girl. It's laid on us not in droppers but in oceans

and hurricanes, in red-sky mornings. But there you are,
little monster of myself. No lifeboat needed. You've learned to swim.

vii.

A pocket of Gushers; the millennial child's favorite sweet. Bottled
breath. Preserved skins of the sea; flounder, bass, and carp. Sucrose.

Naturally Flavored Bullies in a Cup: just add boiling water. Sugared raindrops with jellied chia seeds. Broiled oyster husks. Braised barnacles. Dried Gracilaria on wheat toast with potato chips and crab cakes poached in salmon oil. Octopus sucker soup, beak silenced, and the one eye tossed in the puddle behind your home.

viii.

You are becoming bitter like your mother.
        So many see hate and think it's a competition.
If you listen to them, you will start to think it, too.

So badly, I want to preserve the innocence
        I see leaking away like it's nothing.

Perhaps those are actually my tears, my wishes,
        my regrets. You sneak a swig of whiskey from the pantry,
and there on the kitchen floor falls a cupful.

You fight a girl at school for the first time—
        she threw things into your hair—and suddenly

you can house a small guppy for a pet. You smoke
        something you shouldn't after band practice and my god,
I'll never stop loving you but you're gathering

your own clouds now. What sheds from your body
        looks like kelp the color of dying roses. I pick them up
in trails where you walk and save them like baby teeth.
        Soon enough, you'll sprout scales and dive for depths
even I have yet to formally gives names to. Teach me

again how to be brave like you, silver swimmer.
        I'll not let you dive alone again. Like father did.

Show me again what I need not fear after we have
        threaded ourselves through the murmurations
of mackerel, after we can speak the syncopations

of swordfish. This will be us from now on:
      trickster in the river, blesser of bodies,

shaper of fissures. Slick as a gill, we vault
      the water like mullet leap, like a shuttler of salt;
down, downing, downer again, pining always for release.

NOTES

"Fatal" is modeled after Beth Bachmann's poem, "Paternoster."

"Reverse Abuse" is inspired by Matt Rasmussen's poem, "Reverse Suicide."

"Lucretia" is inspired by the oil painting, "Tarquin and Lucretia," completed by Titan in 1571, when the artist was in his eighties, for Philip II of Spain. This painting is now in the Kunsthistorisches Museum in Vienna.

"Lightweaver": The line, "he thumbed through her," is modeled after Sara Henning's brilliant poem, "Terra Inferna," from the line, "the way a man might thumb through a woman." The term "shock wave units" refers to Extracorporeal Shock Wave Lithotripsy Units (ESWL) which is a crucial component that allows medical imaging to go mobile.

"The Music in Silence": The line, "If silence is rest and rest is music," references the word "rest" as a musical term. "Rests" are intervals of silence in pieces of music, marked by symbols indicating the length of the silence.

"Pillars of Salt, Pillars of Ghosts": Section I of this poem pays homage to Sara Henning's poem "Good Kissing," specifically the line: "Lot's wife's a salt goddess. Her body no Sodom, torched." The term, "Hammer of Sol," while also a biblical reference, pays homage to the beloved video game, Destiny 2, as well as the term "sunbreaker," and "Whisperer of the Worm." Section II of this poem references the Broadway musical, *Hadestown*, cited:

> Mitchell, Anaïs, et al. Hadestown / Anaïs Mitchell. Righteous Babe Records, 2010.

"Golden Shovel": A Golden Shovel is a poetic form in which the last word of each line forms a second, pre-existing poem (or section thereof). This poem pays homage to Beth Bachmann's poem, "Setting," with her line reading: "A lilac can hold on, half-dead, for days…"

"Things I Inherited from My Father, According to a Mother Before Her Glass of Wine" echoes the structure and sentiment of Jennifer Espinoza's poem, "Things That Make Me Feel Embarrassed."

"How It Feels to Lose Someone" is inspired by Jack Gilbert's famous poem, "Michiko Dead."

"Poem to the Unnameable Father" pays homage to Dorothea Lasky's "Poem to an Unnameable Man."

👁 Poems marked with this symbol are meant to be read alongside a special aspect of this collection: a collaboration which features original artworks created by talented visual artists, each inspired by the themes and emotions of the selected poems. The aim of this project is to create an immersive, multi-sensory experience that enhances the connection between words and images. Please visit my website at https://laurencrawfordpoet.com to view the virtual gallery where the artwork is displayed.

Special thanks are given to the participating artists:

Oormila Vijayakrishnan Prahlad portrayed the poem, "Galveston." Prahlad is an Indian-Australian artist, poet, and improv pianist who was raised in the Middle East. She holds a Masters in English, and is a member of Sydney's North Shore Poetry Collective. She was a founding editor of the Sydney based literary journal Authora Australis. Her works have been widely published in various print and online literary journals and anthologies including, *Cordite Poetry Review, Bracken Magazine, Sidhe Press* (Germany), and *Black Bough Poetry* (UK). Her poetry and art have been nominated for a Pushcart Prize and multiple times for the Sundress Best of the Net Awards Anthology.

She is the author of three digital micro chapbooks published by Origami Poems Project, US. Her debut collection, *Patchwork Fugue*, was published by Atomic Bohemian Press, UK, in February 2024. She lives and works in New South Wales on the traditional lands of The Eora Nation. Her work can be found at https://poetry.oormila.com.

Leslie Landau portrayed the poem, "The Mullet Leap." Landau earned her BFA in printmaking/drawing from The Ohio State University, and graduate gertification, MS in art education and 6th year in educational leadership from Central Connecticut State University. Her work has been included in many exhibitions across Connecticut and New York, including Mattatuck Museum, New Britain Museum of American Art, Connecticut Academy of Art, Silvermine Art Guild, Emerge Gallery, and Five Points Gallery. She was the recipient of the Philanthropic Institute's Artist Renewal Grant, which culminated in a presentation of new work at the New Britain Museum of Art. Her work is held in private collections throughout New England, New York, Ohio, Washington, and California. Leslie is represented by Switch Gallery, Bantam, Connecticut, and Hen's Nest Gallery, Washington Depot, Connecticut. Her work can be found at https://www.lesliealandau.com/.

Katherine Saltoun portrayed the poem, "Artichoke." Saltoun is an artist currently based in Brooklyn, New York. Her work has been exhibited in galleries throughout the United States, England, and Edinburgh. Katie's work explores a mother's energy, strength, and complex mindset. It is a reflection of her experiences as a mother of three young children. She works with mediums and processes such as paper, ink, pen, intaglio, chine colle', collage, and photography. She is drawn to black and white images to simplify the complex relationship that a mother has with themselves and their child(ren). She received her BFA in painting and drawing from the University of Michigan, an MA in art education from Columbia University, and she will become a 2025 graduate from the Pratt Institute with an MFA in painting & drawing. Her work can be found at https://www.katieheller-saltoun.com/.

YERANG MOON portrayed the poem, "The Music in Silence." Moon (b.1999, Seoul, Korea) is an artist currently based in New York as a Fulbright scholar. Driven by a curiosity about how individuals become collectives, she explores the dynamics of our lives. She makes paintings, high reliefs, and installations to delve into the complex relationship between individuals and society by metaphorically exploring in 2D and 3D the visible and nonvisible aspects of humans. Before pursuing her MFA at the Pratt Institute (expected date of graduation, May 2025), Yerang received a BFA from Seoul National University in 2021. She had a solo show ("Solid or Liquid") at Mora Museum in Jersey City in August 2024. Also, she participated in the following selected group shows: "International Exhibition" at Awita New York Studio in New York, "980617-2" at Rainbow Cube Gallery and "X Being X and Not X at the Same Time" at Woosuk Gallery in Korea. In May 2024, she was selected as a resident artist in Cellar Artist Run Residency in Brooklyn, New York. Two group exhibitions and the Los Angeles Art Residency program in the United States are scheduled this year. Her work can be found at https://www.moonyerang.com/.

ACKNOWLEDGMENTS

Special thanks are given to my mentors, Sara Henning, Allison Joseph and Judy Jordan for seeing me, guiding me, and molding me. Thank you so much for your kindness, acceptance and encouragement.

This book would not exist without the support of Southern Illinois University, Carbondale's MFA program. I offer my appreciation to my cohort, whose diligent feedback was immensely helpful. Thank you for pushing me to be better.

Thank you to my editor at Cornerstone Press, Eva Nielsen; publisher Dr. Ross Tangedal; and the entire press team at the University of Wisconsin Stevens–Point for making this book possible, and for your commitment to publishing literature.

Thank you to the Willie Morris Awards, the faculty of the University of Mississippi, and especially to Susan Kinsolving for choosing my poetry for the award, and for your subsequent friendship. Thank you to all who honored me at the Oxford Conference for the Book, particularly Susan Nicholas, David Rae Morris, Susanne Dietzel, Dave & Reba White Williams, David Crews, January Gill O'Neil, Saddiq Dzukogi, David Joy, Cassandra Jackson, Shaundi Wall, and Molly Goldwasser.

I am grateful to my support system: Janet Carr, Robbie Averett, Brendon Averett, Johnette Downing, John Downing, Christina Norris, Benjamin Kobeski, Alexis Sears, Clay Stockton, Hinatsa, Dustin Brookshire, Kimberly Verhines, Mark Sanders, and Nicole Fanaff.

I give my gratitude to my life partner, Ryan Crawford. Thank you for the life we continue to build together.

LAUREN CRAWFORD earned an MFA in poetry from Southern Illinois University, Carbondale. A native of Houston, Texas, she is the recipient of the 2023 Willie Morris Award. Her poetry has either appeared or is forthcoming in *Best New Poets, Poet Lore, Passengers Journal, Prime Number Magazine, SoFloPoJo, The Florida Review, Red Ogre Review, Ponder Review, The Midwest Quarterly, THIMBLE, The Worcester Review, The Spectacle,* and elsewhere. Lauren serves on the editorial teams of Iron Oak Editions and Palette Poetry. Connect with her @laurencraw.bsky.social

www.ingramcontent.com/pod-product-compliance
Lightning Source LLC
Chambersburg PA
CBHW030509130626
46549CB00007B/2914